First World War
and Army of Occupation
War Diary
France, Belgium and Germany

38 DIVISION
Divisional Troops
Divisional Cyclist Company
2 December 1915 - 10 May 1916

WO95/2545/2

The Naval & Military Press Ltd
www.nmarchive.com
Published in association with The National Archives

Published by

The Naval & Military Press Ltd

Unit 10 Ridgewood Industrial Park,

Uckfield, East Sussex,

TN22 5QE England

Tel: +44 (0) 1825 749494

www.naval-military-press.com

www.nmarchive.com

This diary has been reprinted in facsimile from the original. Any imperfections are inevitably reproduced and the quality may fall short of modern type and cartographic standards.

© Crown Copyright
Images reproduced by permission of The National Archives, London, England, 2015.

Contents

Document type	Place/Title	Date From	Date To
Heading	WO95/2545/2		
Heading	38th Division 38th Divl Cyclist Coy Dec 1915-May 1916 To II Corps		
Heading	38th Divl Cyclist Vol I 121/7824		
War Diary		02/12/1915	20/12/1915
Heading	38th Cyclist Vol 2 Jan 16		
War Diary	St Venant	01/01/1916	11/01/1916
War Diary	Lacouture	11/01/1916	17/01/1916
War Diary	Locon	21/01/1916	31/01/1916
Heading	38th Cyclist Vol 3		
War Diary	Locon	01/02/1916	29/02/1916
War Diary	Essars Pas de Calais	00/03/1916	01/04/1916
War Diary	Therouanne	02/04/1916	02/04/1916
War Diary	Hesdin L'abbe	03/04/1916	17/04/1916
War Diary	Therouanne	18/04/1916	30/04/1916
Heading	War Diary Of 38th Div (Welsh) Cyclist Coy From 1-5-16 To 10-5-16 Volume 5		
War Diary	Lestrem	01/05/1916	10/05/1916
War Diary	Wittes	10/05/1916	10/05/1916

WO 95/25412

38TH DIVISION

38TH DIVL CYCLIST COY.
DEC 1915 - MAY 1916

TO II CORPS

38ʳᵈ Stil: Cyclists-
Vol: I

121/3844

Dec '15
May '16

Army Form C. 2118.

WAR DIARY
or
INTELLIGENCE SUMMARY.
(Erase heading not required.)

38th (Welsh) Divisional Cyclist Company.

Instructions regarding War Diaries and Intelligence Summaries are contained in F.S. Regs., Part II. and the Staff Manual respectively. Title pages will be prepared in manuscript.

Hour, Date, Place	Summary of Events and Information	Remarks and references to Appendices
9. am 2nd December 1915	Left Winchester for Active Service.	
5 pm " 3rd "	Entrained at Southampton.	
7 am " 3rd December 1915	Disembarked at Havre went into Rest Camp.	
6 am 5th " "	Entrained at Havre.	
9 pm 6th " "	Arrived at GLOMINGHEM via AIRE went into billets	
10 am 8th " "	Left GLOMINGHEM went into billets at ENGUINEGATTE.	
8. am 20th " "	Left ENGUINEGATTE went into billets at ST VENANT.	

Robert Userell Jones .... O.C.
38th (Welsh) Divisional Cyclist Company.

38½ Tycho
Tol: 2
Jan '16

Army Form C. 2118.

WAR DIARY for January 1916

or

INTELLIGENCE SUMMARY.

(Erase heading not required.)

Instructions regarding War Diaries and Intelligence Summaries are contained in F. S. Regs., Part II. and the Staff Manual respectively. Title pages will be prepared in manuscript.

HEADQUARTERS
No. CC/0/
31 JAN 1916
38th (WELSH) DIVISIONAL CYCLIST COMPANY

Hour, Date, Place	Summary of Events and Information	Remarks and references to Appendices
January 1st – 11th ST VENANT	Continued work - throwing & wiring Breastworks & wire reconnaissance. Also supplied working fatigue parties daily for trench boards, loopholes, trench parapets.	
January 11th LACOUTURE	Company less two platoons proceeded to billets in Gare Street LACOUTURE & carried on drainage work of Scheme which had been commenced by 19th Div Cy Coy. Co sent platoon left at ST VENANT with exception of two coys. wound under brick & bomb fatigues.	
January 17th LACOUTURE	Company on return from ST VENANT to No 6 Platoon which had been on of the two platoons left at rear relief plans.	
January 24th LOCON	moved to billets at LOCON.	
January 25th LOCON	The ST VENANT detachment of 2 platoons rejoined Co. Company at LOCON	
January 26th – 31st LOCON	Drainage work in trenches under haches supervised on Jan 17th reconnoitred under direction of C.R.E. 38th Division.	

O. Percy Davies Fr. O.C.
38th (Welsh) Divisional
Cyclist Company.

38th Cyclops
Vol: 3

Army Form C. 2118.

WAR DIARY
or
INTELLIGENCE SUMMARY.
(Erase heading not required.)

29 FEB 1916

Hour, Date, Place	Summary of Events and Information	Remarks and references to Appendices
February 15th LOCON to Feby 15th	Day & night working parties supplied to 123rd Welsh Coy.R.E. for work on communication trenches & drainage in S.15. (ref map BETHUNE Contours sheet 36A x 36B)	Letter a/alk 3/2/16 O.C. 123rd Wels Coy. R.E.
February 18th	Moved to new billets in ESSARS X.25.A. (ref map as above)	38th Divl Operation Order No 9 Branch Table No. 221
February 23rd/29th	Day & night working parties supplied to 151 Wels Coy. R.E. on communication trenches at GIVENCHY A.9.C. ref map as above	G.S. mg dated 22/2/16 from O.C. 151st Welsh Coy R.E.

Robert Elbanell Capt. O.C.
38th (Welsh) Divisional
Cyclist Company.

38 DW
Cyclists
Vol 4

38th (Welsh) Divisional Cyclist Company.

Army Form C.2118.

WAR DIARY
or
INTELLIGENCE SUMMARY.
(Erase heading not required.)

Instructions regarding War Diaries and Intelligence Summaries are contained in F.S. Regs., Part II. and the Staff Manual respectively. Title pages will be prepared in manuscript.

HEADQUARTERS No. OC 13/6/4 ≡ 1 APR 1916 38th (WELSH) DIVISIONAL CYCLIST COMPANY

Hour, Date, Place	Summary of Events and Information	Remarks and references to Appendices
ESSARS PAS de CALAIS. March 1916.	Continued to supply working parties during the month of March to work under OC 151st Field Coy RE at GIVENCHY.	

Robert Munn Capt......O.C.
38th (Welsh) Divisional
Cyclist Company.

Army Form C. 2118.

Vol 5

XXXVIII WAR DIARY or INTELLIGENCE SUMMARY.

(Erase heading not required.)

HEADQUARTERS
No. GC 43/2/2
30 APR 1916
88th (WELSH) DIVISIONAL CYCLISTS

Hour, Date, Place	Summary of Events and Information	Remarks and references to Appendices
10. am 1/4/16 ESSARS	Company marched to THEROUANNE arriving 1/2.	Our wire Q 968 March 29/16.
8. am 2/4/16 THEROUANNE	Company proceeded to HESDIN L'ABBÉ near SAMER arriving there the same.	
April 3rd HESDIN L'ABBÉ to April 16th	Company was thoroughly instructed in minor tactics at Divl. MOUNTED TROOPS SCHOOL of 1st CAVALRY DIVISION.	
8 am April 17th HESDIN L'ABBÉ to LESTREM	Company returned to THEROUANNE arriving the evening of April 17/16.	
8. am April 18th THEROUANNE	Company marched & went into billets.	Our wire A 454 25/4/16 Our letter No 9 S 29/10/4 B 25/4/16
April 19th to April 30th	Company went into day working parties to "B" Branch of Divsn. at ESTAIRES. Work of night patrols at 103rd Field Co RE & at Bombs at LAVENTIE.	

D. Percy Davies Capt. O.O.
88th (Welsh) Divisional
Cyclist Company

Cyclists 38 Div
vol 6

CONFIDENTIAL

WAR DIARY
of
38th Div (WELSH) Cyclist Coy

From 1.5.16 To 10.5.16

(VOLUME 6)

WAR DIARY
INTELLIGENCE SUMMARY.
(Erase heading not required.)

Army Form C. 2118.

Hour, Date, Place	Summary of Events and Information	Remarks and references to Appendices
LESTREM May 1st to 6.10½	Supplied working parties day & night to "Q" Branch 38th Divn and 123rd Field Coy R.E. On alternate days provided afsn warfare. instr. O.C. 38th Divn Mounted Troops.	Divl Circ #479 Verbal instructional.
May 10th	Left LESTREM and reported to O.C. XIth Corps Cyclist Battn at WITTES.	XIth Corps Q.M. 3 & 38th (Welsh) Divn order No 25.
WITTES May 10th	Company transferred from 38th Divn to XIth Corps and became No 3 Coy XIth Corps Cyclist Battn.	

D. Percy Davies Capt. O.C.
38th (Welsh) Divisional
Cyclist Company.

www.ingramcontent.com/pod-product-compliance
Lightning Source LLC
Chambersburg PA
CBHW081254170426
43191CB00037B/2158